# Interiors  Yellow

ROCKPORT PUBLISHERS
GLOUCESTER, MASSACHUSETTS

Copyright © 1998 by Rockport Publishers, Inc.

All rights reserved. No part of this book may be reproduced in any form without written permission of the copyright owners. All images in this book have been reproduced with the knowledge and prior consent of the artists concerned and no responsibility is accepted by producer, publisher, or printer for any infringement of copyright or otherwise, arising from the contents of this publication. Every effort has been made to ensure that credits accurately comply with information supplied.

First published in the United States of America by:
Rockport Publishers, Inc.
33 Commercial Street
Gloucester, Massachusetts  01930-5089
Telephone: (978) 282-9590
Facsimile: (978) 283-2742

Distributed to the book trade and art trade in the United States by:
North Light Books, an imprint of
F & W Publications
1507 Dana Avenue
Cincinnati, Ohio  45207
Telephone: (800) 289-0963

Other Distribution by:
Rockport Publishers, Inc.
Gloucester, Massachusetts  01930-5089

ISBN 1-56496-444-2

10 9 8 7 6 5 4 3 2 1

Designer: Karen Rappaport
Cover Image: Photo by Sam Gray
            See page 91

Printed in Hong Kong by Midas Printing Limited.

For more beautiful work by the designers and photographers featured in this collection, please see:

*Showcase of Interior Design: Eastern Edition 1*
*Showcase of Interior Design: Eastern Edition 2*
*Showcase of Interior Design: Eastern Edition 3*
*Showcase of Interior Design: Midwest Edition 1*
*Showcase of Interior Design: Midwest Edition 2*
*Showcase of Interior Design: Pacific Edition 1*
*Showcase of Interior Design: Pacific Edition 2*
*Showcase of Interior Design: Southern Edition 1*
*Showcase of Interior Design: Southern Edition 2*
*Colors for Living: Bedrooms* by Carol Meredith
*Colors for Living: Living Rooms* by Jennie Pugh
*Eclectic Style in Interior Design* by Carol Meredith

The neutrality of yellow sometimes belies its importance in the color scheme of a room. Pale yellows will add warmth to a room otherwise stark in its whiteness, yet yellow is neutral enough to showcase the more daring colors in the room. Though yellow can recede into the background, it just as easily can become the focal point: Think of a bright yellow sunburst on a dark background. From pale, sandy yellow to bright tulip yellow to glittery gold, the opportunities and choices for using the color yellow in a room's color palette are infinite. Sunshine yellow brings happiness to a room. Pair yellow with purple for a royal effect. Primary yellow energizes when combined with red and blue. Sometimes yellow in a room is not from purposeful color choices, rather, our incandescent lighting has yellow undertones, giving a glowing, warm cast to a room. This warm, cozy atmosphere can be further enhanced with yellow walls and accessories. Yellow, in any shade or tone, is perfect for every room of the house. Mix and match it: the opportunities are yours!

(above) Designed for a man with eclectic tastes, a non-traditional color scheme complements the mix of traditional and modern furniture in this study/bedroom.

INTERIOR DESIGN

*Interior Options*

(right) INTERIOR DESIGN

*Sheila Britz Design, Inc.*

(above) This superb living room hosts an exuberant meeting of classical, rococo, and contemporary styles. Note how the fabrics and upholstery alternate between the past and present.

INTERIOR DESIGN

*Barry Dixon*

*Photo: Gordon Beall*

(above) A lively floral pattern makes a splash in this vibrant family room. The walls and furniture create an intimate atmosphere emphasizing relaxed formality—a reflection of the client's lifestyle and personality.

(left) Combined with detailed architectural paneling, the floral wallcovering appears to be clinging from a garden trellis.

INTERIOR DESIGN

*V-3 Design*

*(above)* Combine pastels with intense, dark color to create a room of lively contrasts. Here, the butter-colored walls and pastel upholstery are the perfect foil for the highly colored and patterned rug and dark wood finishings.

INTERIOR DESIGN
*Richard Fitzgerald*

*Photo: Steve Vierra*

(above) INTERIOR DESIGN

Barry Dixon

Photo: Gordon Beall

(above) A very small living room in a carriage house presented the challenge of making use of existing furniture. A periwinkle blue ceiling and linen-colored walls create a palette that easily blends with all colors.

INTERIOR DESIGN

*Elizabeth Read Weber, ASID*

*(left)* INTERIOR DESIGN

*Jane Crary Interior Design*

*(above)* A bejeweled daffodil-yellow
and red room enhances a superb art
and antique collection, making for a
dramatic room day and night.

INTERIOR DESIGN
*James R. Irving, ASID*

(above) INTERIOR DESIGN

Barbara Lazarus

(above) All furniture by Letelier & Rock is custom-made for this room. Linen scrims at the windows are also by Letelier & Rock. The room features ashwood and steel lamps, brushed steel sconces, ashwood sofas with zip-off cushions, and bookcases.

INTERIOR DESIGN
*Letelier & Rock Design, Inc.*

(right) Classical elements play beautifully in this living and dining room in shades of warm white—private residence, Constance Woolsey, Nashville, Tennessee.

INTERIOR DESIGN
*G. S. Hinsen Company*

(above) INTERIOR DESIGN

James R. Irving, ASID

(above) Like the sun in the sky, blue and yellow
are a natural combination. Here, prints, patterns,
and objects from around the world draw attention
to an intimate space of warm and cool, sunny
and subdued colors.

INTERIOR DESIGN

Ann Sullivan

Photo: Steve Vierra

*(below)* Mauve pink walls and a lovely English floral fabric, Carlotta, offset a superb collection of rare and important antiques and give a sense of serenity.

INTERIOR DESIGN
*James R. Irving, ASID*

18

(above) INTERIOR DESIGN

omar Lampert Associates

hoto: Chuck White

(above) New construction was given
an old world feel by richly glazing
walls, and using heavy textured fabrics
in this den and library—private residence, Mr. and Mrs. Don Ware,
Abbotsford, Nashville, Tennessee.

INTERIOR DESIGN
*G. S. Hinsen Company*

(right)  Cheerful furnishings create an
aura of casual elegance without detrac
ing from the room's striking architecture

INTERIOR DESIGN
*Diane Wendell Interior Design*

(above) The rich color tapestry on the
walls coordinates with the elegant
antique Oriental rug to give this room
texture. Deep, plush window treatments
enhance the relaxed, but traditional,
interior.

INTERIOR DESIGN
*Akins and Aylesworth, Ltd.*

*(above)* Glazed pale lemon makes this San Francisco living room sunny even on the foggiest days. A smattering of Oriental floral chintz from Clarence House adds to the colors in the impressionist and contemporary paintings. The Ihurrie carpet helps maintain a contemporary point of view, but the furnishings are a mix of traditional and modern styles.

INTERIOR DESIGN

*Mario Buatta Incorporated*

(above) INTERIOR DESIGN

*Antine Associates Interior Design*

(above) An adult, city apartment has soaring views of Central Park. The pale colors and selected antiques give a soft and stable background to daily life with treetop views. Originally a two-story artist's studio, the balcony now serves as the master bedroom.

INTERIOR DESIGN

David Ripp Incorporated

INTERIOR DESIGN

*Clifford Stiles McAlpin Interiors, Inc.*

*(right)* INTERIOR DESIGN

*Oetgen Design and Fine Antiques, Inc.*

(above) The warmth of the room is achieved by using
a mixture of elegant fabrics, fine antiques and collectibles, and wonderfully comfortable upholstery. The
chinoise secretary is seventeenth century, the bull's eye
mirror eighteenth century, and the rug late nineteenth
century. The walls are upholstered in Scottish wool
woven in a Russian pattern.

INTERIOR DESIGN

*Antine Associates*

INTERIOR DESIGN

*Clifford Stiles McAlpin Interiors, Inc.*

(above) INTERIOR DESIGN

*Coulson-Hamlin*

(right) The parlour of historic Sweetbrush Estate, Austin, Texas (1852) in its happiest palette of its 140 years. Lead print fabric—Brunschwig-Fils.

INTERIOR DESIGN

*Nicholson Interiors*

*(above)* INTERIOR DESIGN

*Jane Crary Interior Design*

(above) Reading or relaxing by the fire on a
"tete-a-tete" designed by Antine—formality
with a huge accent on comfort.

INTERIOR DESIGN

*Antine Associates*

(above) Sophisticated with its
mix of formal and country antique
pieces, this charming weekend retreat
incorporates cheerful fabrics and
persian rugs.

INTERIOR DESIGN

*Ellen Korney Associates*

*eft)* INTERIOR DESIGN

*cki Tucker Interiors and Cabin Antiques*

(above) This end of a formal living room opens onto a covered loggia, allowing an unusual blending of indoor and outdoor furnishings, including a fire screen fashioned from a garden gate. Mirrored surfaces add light and space.

INTERIOR DESIGN

Barry Dixon, Inc.

(left) Elegance is carefully balanced with the help of a French screen, Italian console and chintz slipcovered chairs.

INTERIOR DESIGN
Rodgers Menzies Interior Design

(below) INTERIOR DESIGN
Creative Decorating

Photo: David Livingston

(above) INTERIOR DESIGN

*Anne Weinberg Designs, Inc.*

(above) INTERIOR DESIGN

Robert Pope Associates, Inc.

(above) The sleeping porch of
"Leighton," *The Fred Rand House.*

INTERIOR DESIGN

*Sanford R. Thigpen Interiors, Inc.*

(below) INTERIOR DESIGN

Kathy Harman/The Corner Cupboard Antiques and Interiors

(above) Designing beautiful interiors requires
magnificent sources, attention to detail and the
ability to capture the essence of the client's dreams,
as shown in this elegant traditional interior. The
feature of the room is the antique eighteenth
century Aubusson rug. Antique furnishings and
accessories were collected from France and
England and are blended with luxurious fabrics,
upholstery and contemporary art.

INTERIOR DESIGN

*Ann Platz & Co.*

(right) Timeless elegance fills the living
room of this 6,000 square foot New
York apartment that had been gutted
prior to renovation.

INTERIOR DESIGN

*V-3 Design*

(above) Walls, ceilings, moldings and columns
form a background against which the best of
the old is combined with the best of the new.

INTERIOR DESIGN
*V-3 Design*

*(left and below)* INTERIOR DESIGN

*Ricki Tucker Interiors and Cabin Antiques*

*(below)* A golden master suite, spare yet elegant,
serves as an inviting private retreat in this Palm
Beach, Florida, home.

INTERIOR DESIGN

*Stedila Design, Inc.*

(above) A bedroom writing area features stenciled
and glazed walls, a Louis XVI writing table and
painted eighteenth century open armchairs.

INTERIOR DESIGN
Joanne De Palma, Inc.

(below) INTERIOR DESIGN

James R. Irving, ASID

(right) The living room of a Greek Revival
cottage in Florida reflects the owner's love
of color and design.

INTERIOR DESIGN

Clifford Stiles McAlpin Interiors, Inc.

*(above)* The grand living room of a Hudson River property projects designer Barbara Ostrom's ability to recreate period architecture, cabinetry, columns and moldings while orchestrating color and texture, fabrics and furnishings, in a large scale setting.

INTERIOR DESIGN

*Barbara Ostrom Associates, Inc.*

*(left)* This Palm Beach living room encompasses the various styles of the client's collections.

INTERIOR DESIGN

*Barbara Lazarus*

(right) INTERIOR DESIGN

Muriel Hebert, Inc.

(above) The herringbone wood floor and antique
rug highlight a medley of patterns and textures.

INTERIOR DESIGN

*Deutsch/Parker Design Ltd.*

*bove)* Antiques accent a space that
*x*udes a cutting-edge attitude.

TERIOR DESIGN

*eya Serabian*

*oto: Steve Vierra*

(left) INTERIOR DESIGN

*Barbara Lazarus*

*left)* The Kips Bay Showhouse in New York boasts
an atelier bridge of steel and aluminum grille,
accessed by hidden stairs behind the cracked-plas-
er wall. Indicative of the Stedila Design style is the
mixture of classic furnishings with contemporary
materials and architectural details.

INTERIOR DESIGN

Stedila Design, Inc.

(above) French furnishings and architectural
details add grandeur to a spacious sitting
area. Note the custom cord and tassels on
the French empire sofa.

INTERIOR DESIGN

*Edward C. Turrentine Interior Design Inc.*

(above) Along the side of a formal room, a canted mirror casually reflects as much light and space as the flanking windows. A custom plaster ceiling is painted like the wall and trim for unity and height.

INTERIOR DESIGN

Barry Dixon, Inc.

*(above)* Inspiring design elements
breathe character into a functional
space that's conducive to creativity
and reflection.

INTERIOR DESIGN
*Judith Lynne Interior Design*

*(right)* INTERIOR DESIGN

*Ellen Sosnow Interiors*

(above) This living room evolved after a renovation of a newly empty nest household. The client wanted a comfortable room with abundant seating capacity. Bookcases were added for symmetry and to showcase the client's collectibles, art, and family photographs. Bright colors were used throughout.

INTERIOR DESIGN

Rita St. Clair Associates, Inc.

(above) Bright, comfortable and inviting, this living room makes dramatic use of textures, colors and furniture styles.

(left) Elegant antique furnishings greet guests with a traditional welcome in this foyer.

INTERIOR DESIGN
*Sirola Designs, Ltd.*

(above) INTERIOR DESIGN

James R. Irving, ASID

*eft)* New construction is given the feeling of

200-year-old manor house with the addition

*f* a stone wall and beautifully oiled dark walnut

*oors*. The French Bressane armoire in walnut

*url* and cherry, circa 1820, and beautiful

*ubusson* rug further this look of an age rich

*ith* tradition.

*NTERIOR DESIGN*

*Meadowbank Designs, Inc.*

(below) Niche at the end of a hall holds a mahogany George III bonheur de deux jour, a white painted French box, and nineteenth century Wedgwood creamware tweed bowl and vase.

INTERIOR DESIGN

*Joanne DePalma, Inc.*

(right) A collection of family treasures, special objects and antique furniture fill one wall in this elegant living room.

INTERIOR DESIGN

*Sirola Designs Ltd.*

(above) INTERIOR DESIGN

*Lowrance Interiors, Inc.*

*(left)* A rich balance of warm colors, textures, fabrics and furnishings combines to give this jewelry store an ambiance of gracious luxury.

INTERIOR DESIGN

*SPACES/Interior Design*

*Photo: John C. Lindy*

(left) The owner's multitude of collections and love of color are expressed.

(below left) A porch is now correspondence, game and bar multifunctions.

INTERIOR DESIGN

*Klingmans of Grand Rapids*

(right) Crisp marble floors and glass blocks create a dramatic backdrop for a formal contemporary dining area.

INTERIOR DESIGN

*Tomar Lampert Associates*

(above) The owners of this pied-a-terre have an extensive contemporary art collection, including a three-dimensional painting by Arman, and bronze sculpture by Anthony Caro.

INTERIOR DESIGN
*Carl Steele Associates, Inc.*

(left) Combined with detailed architectural paneling, the floral wallcovering appears to be clinging from a garden trellis.

INTERIOR DESIGN
*V-3 Design*

(above) The marble-top console buffet took
six years to find because the client had
something specific in mind. The color
scheme was designed around the existing
antique rug and accessories.

INTERIOR DESIGN

*Auer Interior Design*

(above) A charming French folly, this
breakfast room was designed to be a sunny
whimsical pavilion. The chinoiserie lantern
and playful mural characters inspire a
lighthearted morning.

INTERIOR DESIGN

*Samantha Cole & Company*

(above) The golden glazed walls beautifully echo the colors found in the original art glass in this arts and crafts dining room.

INTERIOR DESIGN

*Gail Prauss Interior Design, Inc.*

(right) A fine collection of eighteenth and early nineteenth century English antiques highlight the gilded quality of this sumptuous formal dining room.

INTERIOR DESIGN

*Eberlein Design Consultants Ltd.*

*(below)* Family antiques and warm colors create a cozy environment for fine and casual dining.

INTERIOR DESIGN

*Gail Adams Interiors Ltd.*

*(right)* A candlelight background color brings an extra degree of warmth to the dinner table. The shell corner cabinet becomes a focal point thanks to sponge painting in a contrasting color.

INTERIOR DESIGN

*Barbara Metzler Interior Design, Inc.*

(above) INTERIOR DESIGN

Barbara Jacobs Interior Design

Photo: Russell Abraham

eft) INTERIOR DESIGN

rowns Interiors, Inc.

(above) INTERIOR DESIGN

Robert Stilin, Inc.

(above) Designing beautiful interiors requires magnificent sources, attention to detail and the ability to capture the essence of the client's dreams, as shown in this elegant traditional interior. The feature of the room is the antique eighteenth century Aubusson rug. Antique furnishings and accessories were collected from France and England and are blended with luxurious fabrics, upholstery and contemporary art.

INTERIOR DESIGN

*Ann Platz & Co.*

(above) The corner of a woman's bedroom in a townhouse done in light colors, contrasted with black lacquered antiques.

INTERIOR DESIGN
*Tonin MacCallum ASID Inc.*

(right) An antique pine headboard, English chintzes and an heriloom quilt highlight this sunny bedroom.

INTERIOR DESIGN
*Diane Alpern Kovacs, Interior Design, Inc.*

*(above)* Lemon walls with off-white moldings frame a
collection of porcelain floral plates and paintings. The
simple dotted Swiss fabric works well with the pink
plaid curtain and bed ensemble. The rose-patterned
carpet sits on green-and-white bow carpeting (both
from Stark). The oval mirror is English. The upholstery is
designed by Mario Buatta for John Widdicomb
Company and covered in fabrics from Brunschwig and
Fils.

INTERIOR DESIGN
*Mario Buatta Incorporated*

(above) Collections of heirloom family photographs
add a welcome sense of personal history to any home.
On this bedroom wall, the images are matted against
various floral backgrounds in identical gold frames to
create a unique display. The rest of the room is a
charming blend of antiques gathered over the years.

INTERIOR DESIGN

Kenneth Hockin Interior Decoration

Photo: William Stites

(above) INTERIOR DESIGN

Anne Weinberg Designs, Inc.

(above) Pale colors get a boost from the gilded surfaces of furniture and the metallic sheen of drapery and
upholstery fabrics. The resulting glow of ambient light
quietly enlivens this subtle, restful palette.

*Photo: Richard Mandelkorn*

*(below)* A mix of eight patterns in a palette of yellow, marigold, blue, and white creates a cheerful but not busy scheme. No wall long enough to accept a queen bed necessitated the placement of the bed in the center of the room.

INTERIOR DESIGN

*Interior Options*

(above) Neutral schemes are ideal for bringing artwork and
the shapes and textures of furnishings into sharp relief.
When planning a neutral color scheme for a bedroom, pay
particular attention to sources of ambient and natural light,
since the play of light and shadow is crucial to a successful
design.

*Photo: Sam Gray*

*(right)* A unique iron bed and bench combine with reproduction wood furnishings and muted florals to provide an interesting, yet relaxing, master bedroom suite.

INTERIOR DESIGN

*J. Powell & Associates, Inc.*

*(right)* INTERIOR DESIGN

*Lowrance Interiors, Inc.*

(above) An antique Chinese textile becomes a unifying
element in a serene master bedroom and commands
the dreamy color palette.

INTERIOR DESIGN
Xolis Betancourt

Akins & Aylesworth, Ltd.
26 E. First Street
Hinsdale, IL 60521
630/325.3355
Fax: 630/325.3315

Ann Platz & Company
Five Piedmont Center
Suite 202
Atlanta, GA 30305
404/237.1000
Fax: 404/237.3810

Anne Weinberg Designs, Inc.
982 Chestnut Run
Gates Mills, OH 44040
440/423.0443
Fax: 440/423.0443

Antine Associates
750 Park Avenue
New York, NY 10021
212/988.4096 or
201/224.0315
Fax: 201/224.5963

Auer Interior Design
300 Cranbrook Road
Bloomfield Hills, MI 48304
248/642.7440
Fax: 248/647.5772

Barbara Jacobs Interior
Design
12340 Saratoga-Sunnyvale
Road
Saratoga, CA 95070
408/446.2225
Fax: 408/446.2607

Barbara Lazarus
10 Fones Alley
Providence, RI 02906
401/521.8910
Fax: 401/438.8809

Barbara Metzler Interior
Design, Inc.
120 Woodley Road
Winnetka, IL 60093
847/501.2929
Fax: 847/501.2923

Barbara Ostrom Associates
1 International Plaza
Mahwah, NJ 07495
201/529.0444
Fax: 201/529.0449
and:
55 East 87th Street
New York, NY 10128
212/465.1808

Barry Dixon, Inc.
2019 Q Street, NW
Washington, DC 20009
202/332.7955
Fax: 202/332.7952

Brown's Interiors, Inc.
1115 Kenilworth Avenue
Charlotte, NC 28204
704/375.2248
Fax: 704/334.0982

Carl Steel Associates, Inc
1606 Pine Street
Philadelphia, PA 19103
215/546.5530
Fax: 215/546.1571

Clifford Stiles McAlpin
Interiors, Inc.
900 East Moreno Street
Pensacola, FL 32503
850/438.8345
Fax: 850/434.8315

The Corner Cupboard
Antiques and Interiors
615 Tuxedo Place, NW
Atlanta, GA 30342
404/231.9655
Fax: 404/231.5916

Coulson-Hamlin
2838 Bellefontaine
Houston, TX 77025
713/666.1620
Fax: 713/666.2410

Creative Decorating
168 Poloke Place
Honolulu, HI
808/955.1465
Fax: 808/943.8450

David Ripp Incorporated
215 West 84th Street
New York, NY 10024
212/362.7706
Fax: 212/362.4486
e-mail: dugancastle@world-
net.att.net

Deutsch/Parker Design, LTD.
325 West Huron Street
Suite 500
Chicago, IL 60610
312/649.1244
Fax: 312/649.9617

Diane Alpern Kovacs, Interior
Design, Inc.
4 Main Street
Roslyn, NY 11576
516/625.0703
Fax: 516/625.8441

Diane Wendell Interior
Design
1121 Warren Avenue
Downers Grove, IL 60515
630/852.0235
Fax: 630/988.8341

Eberlein Design Consultants, Ltd
1809 Walnut Street, Suite 410
Philadelphia, PA 19103
215/405.0400
Fax: 215/405.0588

Edward C. Turrentine Interior
Design, Inc.
70 N. Raymond Avenue
Pasadena, CA 91103
626/795.9964 or
213/681.4221
Fax: 626/795.0027

Ellen Lemer Korney Associate
10170 Culver Blvd.
Culver City, CA 90232
310/204.6576
Fax: 310/204.1457

Elizabeth Read Weber, LLC
79 East Putnam Avenue
Greenwich, CT 06830
203/869.5659
Fax: 203/869,3778
e-mail: erwllc@aol.com

Ellen Sosnow Interiors
850 Park Avenue
New York, NY 10021
212/744.0214
Fax: 212/772.3443

Freya Serabian Design
Associates
36 Church Street
Winchester, MA 01890

Gail Prauss Interior Design Ltd
421 N. Marion Street
Oak Park, IL 60302
708/524.1233
Fax: 708/524.1237

G. S. Hinsen Company
2133 Bandywood Drive
Nashville, TN 37215
615/383.6440
Fax: 615/269.5130

Interior Options
200 Lexington Avenue
New York, NY 10016
212/545.0301
Fax: 212/689.4064

ane Crary Interior Design
784 Park Avenue
New York, NY 10021
212/737.5890
Fax: 212/861.3884

ames R. Irving ASID
3901 Shaker Blvd.
Cleveland, OH 44120
216/283.1991 or
216/751.1100

oanne DePalma Inc.
2109 Broadway, 1570
New York, NY 10023
212/799.6088
ax: 212/799.4014

Powell and Associates Inc.
00 W. Beaver Creek Blvd.
.O. Box 1641
Avon, CO 81620
970/845.7731
ax: 970/845.8903
-mail: jpowell@vail.net

udith Lynne Interior Design
.O. Box 4998
Palm Springs, CA 92263
760/324.7606
ax: 760/328.8190

enneth Hockin Interior
Decoration
Old Chelsea Station
.O. Box 1117
New York, NY 10011

lingmans of Grand Rapids
525 28th Street, SE
Grand Rapids, MI 49512
16/942.7300
ax: 616/942.1957

etelier & Rock Design, Inc.
020 Madison
New York, NY 10021
12/683.5512
ax: 212/683.7608

Lowrance Interiors, Inc.
707 N. Alfred Street
Los Angeles, CA 90069
213/655.9713
Fax: 213/655.0359

Mario Buatta Inc.
120 East 80th Street
New York, NY 10021
212/988.6811
Fax: 212/861.9321

Meadowbank Designs, Inc.
Box 168
Bryn Mawr, PA 19010
610/525.4909
Fax: 610/525.3909

Muriel Hebert Interiors
117 Sheridon Avenue
Piedmont, CA 94611
510/547.1294
Fax: 510/655.1509

Nicholson Interiors
1810 West 35th Street
Austin, TX 78703
512/458.6395
Fax: 512/567.2050

Oetgen Design Inc.
2300 Peachtree Road, NW
Suite B-209
Atlanta, GA 30309
404/352.1112
Fax: 404/352.0505

Ricki Tucker Interiors/Cabin
Antiques
8343 Russell-Topton Road
Meridian, MS 39305
601/679.7921
Fax: 601/484.3225 or
601/679.7200
e-mail: tuck@cybertron.com

Rita St. Clair Associates, Inc.
1009 N. Charles Street
Baltimore, MD 21201
410/752.1313
Fax: 410/752.1335

Robert Pope Associates, Inc.
400 N. Wells Street, #400
Chicago, IL 60610
312/527.2077
Fax: 312/527.2079
e-mail: rpopeassoc@aol.com

Samantha Cole & Company
550 15th Street
San Francisco, CA 94103
415/864.0100
Fax: 415/864.5333

Sanford R. Thigpen
Interiors, Inc
2996 Grandview Avenue
Suite 310
Atlanta, GA 30305
404/351.1411
Fax: 404/240.0558

Sheila Britz Home
1196 Lexington Avenue
New York, NY 10028
212/517.5153
Fax: 212/517.5103

Solis Betancourt
1054 Potomac Street, NW
Washington, DC 20007
202/659.8734
Fax: 202/659.0035

SPACES/Interior Design
4100 Westheimer #239
Houston, TX
713/622.9696
Fax: 713/622.9699
e-mail:
spaces@internet.mci.com

Stedila Design
135 E. 55th Street
New York, NY 10022
212/751.4281
Fax: 212/751.6698

Tomar Lampert Associates
8900 Melrose Avenue
Suite 202
Los Angeles, CA 90069
310/271.4299
Fax: 310/271.1569

Tonin MacCallum ASID Inc.
21 E 90
New York, NY 10128
212/831.8909
Fax: 212/427.2069

V-3 Design
1212 Avenue of Americas
#802
212/222.2551
Fax: 212/222.2201

# ~ Index ~